Glassball Art Projects

Stories of Stone

Stories of Stone

In memory of Jean Gould

First published 2009
by Glassball Art Projects
www.glassball.org.uk

Material from the Tarmac Buxton Lime & Cement Photographic
Archive and Lafarge Aggregates Archive, © 2009. Reproduced
with the kind permission of Tarmac Buxton Lime & Cement and
Lafarge Aggregates.

Designed and typeset by Glassball Art Projects
Printed in the UK by the Cromwell Press Group.

ISBN 978-0-9558060-1-8

Stories of Stone was kindly funded by the Derbyshire Aggregates
Levy Grant Scheme. DALGS is supported by funding from the
Aggregates Levy Sustainability Fund (Defra) through a grant
administered by the Derbyshire Environmental Trust on behalf
of Derbyshire County Council and the Local Area Agreement.

Cover
Tunstead Quarry, 16/12/1955, image courtesy of Tarmac Buxton Lime & Cement

Frontispiece
Cora Glasser, *Inside the social club,* 2008

Opposite
Kerra Holman, *Sterndale Moor in the snow,* 2008

Stories of Stone

Contents

Derbyshire: a county of beautiful scenery, small towns and villages and an honest, working landscape. Thousands of people visit the area each year, making tourism a major industry. The other is quarrying, but how much do any of us who haven't worked in a quarry really know about the industry?

If, for you, the word 'quarry' conjures up a huge plant billowing dust and lorries thundering along Derbyshire's roads, you've only heard part of the story, and that's where *Stories of Stone* comes in. Young people from the area have learned about the history of the quarries by talking with people who have worked in them, some of whose memories span fifty, sixty, seventy years. Others who live near the quarries describe the impact of having 'the plant' just hundreds of metres away. They have visited quarries to see how mechanisation has changed the industry from harsh, back-breaking work in a dirty, dusty environment to the cleaner, sophisticated workplace of today. They've seen how disused areas of quarries have been restored to provide a habitat for birds, animals, flora and fauna, one that is free from the dangers posed by chemicals and man. And they've found out that without the limestone that is described as 'the best in the country', everyone's lives would be very different. From sweets to toothpaste, plastics to steel, bricks to china, limestone is the vital ingredient.

Through the words and photographs of people who really know the quarries and the industry, *Stories of Stone* takes us on a circular journey from the original landscape to the reality of working in a quarry, the mechanisation that changed the industry for ever, and the way environmental issues were dealt with until the land has, once again, returned to the beautiful scenery loved by those who live in and visit Derbyshire.

Jen Edgar
Literature Worker

Tegwyn Holman, *Sterndale Moor with Hindlow Quarry in the background*, 2009

Cora Glasser, *Percy Armitt at his home*, 2008

Introduction and Acknowledgements

Stories of Stone is a response to Derbyshire's industrial quarried landscape. A landscape that has had its structure altered to produce things that we want made.

Stories of Stone aims to explore the social history surrounding these quarrying sites within the High Peak of Derbyshire, and in particular the unique community of Sterndale Moor, whose origination owes itself to the high-quality limestone beneath it. This project wants to celebrate a seldom-heard voice, create an invaluable contemporary record of real lives, and make those rarely discussed experiences available to a wider audience.

The contents of this book represent a selection of what the project group discovered, heard and documented during their time spent over the Autumn and Winter of 2008, leading into 2009. This book is not to be viewed as an academic account of the history of quarrying in the High Peak, but as a collection of glimpses and experiences of those who have, and still do, live and work, in and around this altered landscape.

This book, DVD and accompanying exhibition would not have been possible without the tireless enthusiasm and commitment of the project's volunteers. We and the project's participants would like to thank Sally Nadin and Robin Gray (Derbyshire Environmental Trust), Councillor J. Faulkner, Martha Lawrence (Assistant Museums Manager, Buxton Museum and Art Gallery), Jen Edgar (Literature Worker), Mandy Greenfield (Proofreader) and Geoff Barlow (Print Production Management) for their support and guidance.

Thank you to Frank Emerson, for supervising many quarry visits and providing valuable access to archival material, along with the many Tarmac Buxton Lime & Cement employees who have assisted us during our project. Thank you also to Richard Scott (Quarry Manager, Dowlow) and the many Lafarge Aggregates employees for allowing our group to visit their site and taking an interest in our project. Our special thanks goes to the adult volunteers for allowing us to record their memories and thoughts (a full list of names is supplied at the back of this book).

A special thank you to John and Jean Gould for all their contributions and for working with the young volunteers. We are also grateful to the Sterndale Moor Social Club Committee for hosting this project and helping us with the recruitment of volunteers.

Finally, we would like to thank Alison Tapp for introducing us to Percy Armitt, whose wonderful history of experiences brought archival photographs of this working landscape to life.

Cora Glasser
Project Coordinator, Glassball Art Projects

Tegwyn Holman, *Dowlow Quarry at night*, 2008

Daniel Astill, *Hindlow*, mixed-media collage, 2008

A Brief History of Quarrying around Sterndale Moor

I was born in a village called Chelmorton in 1937. As for most villages in the area, farming was the main occupation and source of income. The other main source of employment was to be found in the local quarries. I was well aware of this from an early age, for my father and many of our neighbours were employed in this industry. Much of the Peak District is located on a bed of high-quality carboniferous limestone, and for thousands of years this resource has been used in one form or another.

It is known that the burning of limestone to make lime can be traced back to Egyptian, Greek and Roman times and you can find evidence of this practice being utilised by local farmers, who had their own crude kilns around the High Peak area, being some of the first in this country to reduce the acidity of their soil with lime.

Before canals and railways were opened and before the invention of the internal combustion engine, farmers and others used to bring their horse-drawn carts to take lime to places in Cheshire, Lancashire, South Yorkshire and Staffordshire, to be used in other manufacturing processes and for improving the soil. The need for stone and lime encouraged the start of small quarries with rather crude kilns incorporated. Many privately owned quarries sprang up in the area, and more and more people were employed to keep up with increasing demand.

One such quarry was set up at Hindlow by a certain Richard Briggs in the 1880s. Most of the employees at this time had to walk to work from Buxton and surrounding villages. At Hindlow a dozen houses were built on site for the employees; this ensured the men were close and could get to their place of work on time, so production was not interrupted. In those early days it was a case of mainly hard manual labour, in a hostile and often dangerous environment, to win the limestone.

In preparation for the drilling process the topsoil and rubble had to be removed using hand tools. Drilling could now take place, done by hand, and then a rather unstable explosive was used to blast out the stone, ready to be broken into the desired sizes. Again this breakage was done by men using hammers and other hand-held tools, and this in turn was again hand-loaded into horse-drawn carts, then later into wagons that moved on rail tracks. This stone was transported to more efficient coal-burning kilns that had been built on site. Lime was then drawn from the kilns and distributed to customers.

Workers at the rock face, Dowlow Quarry, 1937, image courtesy of Lafarge Aggregates

In 1891 thirteen local quarry and lime companies, including Hindlow, amalgamated and formed Buxton Lime Firms Company Limited. As demand further increased going into the 20th century better equipment was provided for its employees, machines such as compressors, air-operated drills and electric generators.

Then along came the First World War of 1914–18. Some of the employees, including my father, went off to war, others had to stay in the quarries, and women were employed to make up for the shortage of men. After the war, female labour mostly ceased in the industry, until required again in the Second World War.

In the middle of the 1920s, Buxton Lime Firms merged with Imperial Chemical Industries Ltd (ICI) to ensure a supply of top-quality stone and lime products to ICI's plants in mid-Cheshire, and new capital was now available for further modernisation. There were some casualties though, as several quarries were closed down, whilst others had new investment.

In the late 1920s, ICI started building alongside the main A515 road, opposite Hindlow Quarry, to provide further housing for its employees. Several stages of building took place until 1950; the village is now called Sterndale Moor. I have lived here now for forty-four years in the same house.

A couple of houses set up as small shops, and horse-drawn carts would come weekly from Buxton and Bakewell, selling fish, vegetables, fruit and bread. In the 1930s a Co-operative store was opened in the village; this supplied virtually all the household needs and thrived for many years.

Hindlow Quarry continued to develop and expand and more people were required to work there; at one time well over 400 men were employed. A social club was built in the village by ICI and officially opened in 1937. The club was a great success, men could relax and have their pint, inter-works games were organised, Christmas handicaps, regular concerts and dances took place, there was a youth club and a St John Ambulance unit based there. A school was set up with three classrooms, a 'golden age' group was formed, and when the Second World War came along in 1939, a Red Cross first-aid station was established there.

Many buses now brought men to work at Hindlow and other quarries, and again women were employed for the duration of the war. After the war there was an ever-increasing demand for limestone, lime and cement to get the country moving once more. Machinery increasingly took over from manual labour, and in the late 1950s Hindlow Quarry's mechanisation programme was completed; this started to reduce

Photograph of quarry workers, including John Gould's father and uncle, image courtesy of John Gould

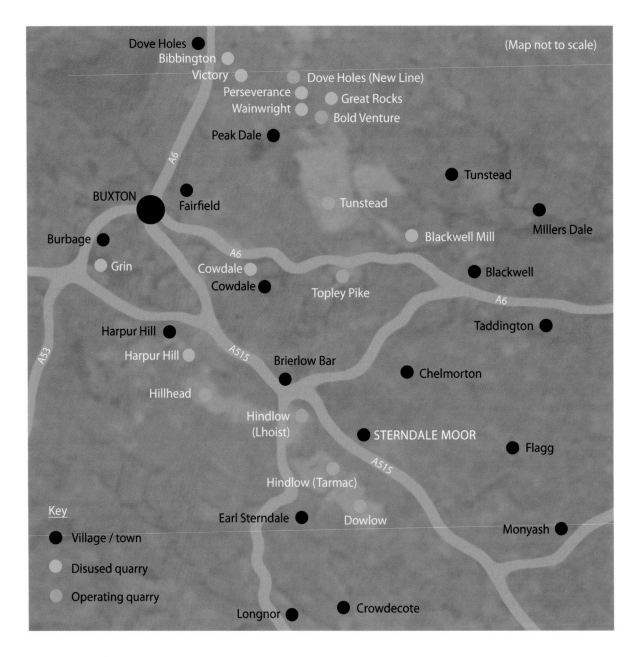

(Map not to scale)

Dove Holes
Bibbington
Victory
Dove Holes (New Line)
Perseverance
Great Rocks
Wainwright
Bold Venture
Peak Dale
Tunstead
BUXTON
Fairfield
Tunstead
Blackwell Mill
MIllers Dale
Burbage
Grin
Cowdale
Cowdale
Topley Pike
Blackwell
Harpur Hill
Taddington
Harpur Hill
Brierlow Bar
Hillhead
Chelmorton
Hindlow
(Lhoist)
STERNDALE MOOR
Flagg
Hindlow (Tarmac)
Earl Sterndale
Dowlow
Monyash

Key
● Village / town
● Disused quarry
● Operating quarry

Longnor
Crowdecote

manning levels. Improvements to the kilns were ongoing and the site was very successful. Maerz gas-fired kilns were commissioned in 1979, but in 1988 a decision was made to stop stone production on the site; stone would now be brought up from ICI's Tunstead site by rail to feed the kilns, which were very efficient at producing high-quality lime with very little waste or pollution. Both Hindlow and Tunstead Quarries are now owned by the Tarmac Group.

The villages of Chelmorton and Sterndale Moor have both seen dramatic and life-changing differences in my lifetime. Only a few people now work at the quarries and all of the houses in Sterndale Moor are now privately owned since ICI decided to sell them off. Every household at one time had at least one, sometimes two or three persons working in the Hindlow Quarry.

What of the future? Well, there are abundant resources of limestone, quarries have a broad base of customers for their products, and hundreds of millions of pounds have been invested on local sites in recent years, with even more proposed. We now have an industry to be proud of. The future is assured.

John Gould
Former Quarry Manager at Tunstead Quarry
Employee of ICI from 1961 to retirement in 1994

Map showing key landmarks and quarries in relation to Sterndale Moor

I was born up here [Burbage, Buxton] near these quarries, in 1907, April. There was no traffic, there was no such thing as tarmac. All the roads were made with what we call chatter, chippings, stone chippings, put on the road with dust and water, I don't know if they put anything else. They had a big steam-roller, it used to take them all day to do about twenty yards of road. In the summer, hot weather, it used to dry up and all the roads were dust. As you walked your shoes were covered with lime dust. They used to have water carts, a two-wheeled cart with a water tanker on with a horse pulling it, and spray the road with water to stop the dust from flying.

I only went to one school, at Burbage. I went when I was five and left when I was thirteen. It was only a small place, not this new one here, up in the village there. When I left I was an errand boy at Leonard's shoe shop on Terrace Road where that flower shop is now. I worked there three years, delivering shoes.

Everybody was in the same boat then. There was nothing. We used to live on rabbits. My dad used to keep a pig and we killed that every year, that carried us on a lot. But you know I used to go to the butcher's for two-pennyworth of bones for making soup.

My dad did the same as me, worked in a quarry. He was a crusher at Hoffman Quarry at Harpur Hill, feeding a crusher. It was terrible.

I lived in a row of cottages, there were ten cottages. We were at number 6. There was no electricity or water. There was one tap, in the middle, opposite our back door, and everybody had to go and fetch the water from this tap. But we didn't have far to go because it was right opposite our back door. Number 5 had six children, we'd five children, next door at number 7 had ten children. So that's twenty-one children and six adults in three houses with two bedrooms.

We used to sleep feet to feet, one at the top, one at the bottom. Terrible. We had a toilet for two houses, outside, an earth lavatory. They used to come and empty them. Buxton Lime owned the properties then and they came every week and emptied them. And they had an ash pit, everybody had coal fires then and had somewhere to throw the ashes and they came and emptied that.

Photograph of pupils at the Sterndale Moor School, image courtesy of Peter Wardle

When the First World War was on there was a German Prisoner of War camp opposite us, right opposite our front door, in the fields. Two of them committed suicide during the four years they were there and they buried them at Burbage churchyard in a separate place. And I always remember, I was a kiddy and went to the funeral and some of the prisoners made wooden crosses for them. That was in 1914 to 1918; I should be seven to eleven. Later on, in the '40s or '50s, they dug them up, these prisoners, and sent them to Germany from Burbage churchyard.

All these prisoners worked in the quarries, Harpur Hill and Grin Quarry.

I always remember the Zeppelins going over and telegraphs coming, people had been killed. A chap put a letter in the *Buxton Advertiser* – did anybody know anything about workmen who worked for Buxton Lime Firms and got killed in the First World War, because there was a memorial in the offices in Spring Gardens at the Royal Exchange? When it closed they'd taken it down to Tunstead, this memorial, with these names on. In this letter in the *Advertiser* he'd put some of these names down and I knew three of them. One of them was my next-door neighbour. I remember, before we went to school, there were no telephones, everything came by telegram, I remember this telegram coming.
[Percy Armitt 24/11/08]

Daniel Astill, *Entrance to Hindlow Quarry*, 2009

I'm Gordon Riley and I live in Buxton, Derbyshire. I was born in Longnor, which is actually in Staffordshire, on the border between Derbyshire and Staffordshire. Most of my father's family was in the quarries although my father was a farmer. He did building labouring in the middle of the day to make a living. The farming wasn't enough, it was only a small-holding.

My first memories of him, he did bearing on the quarries, which was taking the overburden off the top of the stone, at the top of the quarries. He was actually self-employed, using his own horse and cart to carry the soil off the top of the quarry before they blasted the stone.

My mum's ninety-three, ninety-four in April, and bear in mind that when we were harvesting, haymaking, my Mother worked as hard as my father. He'd mow the grass, probably on a Saturday if it was good weather. He wouldn't work on a Sunday, he'd never, ever, go into the hayfield on a Sunday, so Mother would go turning the hay, by hand, whilst my father went off to work. Then, if it was good weather on Tuesday, he'd probably have the day and finish off. And Mother would be going back home doing all the cooking, the washing, everything. Bear in mind she had five children in eight years and she didn't have twins. When she was going haymaking she was loading the children she had at the time onto a pram and pushing them a mile either way, turning the hay, and the smallest field was about an acre. An acre's about the size of two football pitches. A massive area to turn by hand.
[Gordon Riley 05/02/09]

I've got some lovely childhood memories. I remember us going to school and going on nature rambles and playing games. And I used to help my dad. After he'd done a hard day's work at the quarry we used to go at night time and help my brother-in-law's father in the hayfields getting in the crops. In those days, during the war and for a short period afterwards, there was what was called double-summertime. Two hours were altered on the clock, not one, so it used to stay light until midnight to help the farmers get the crops in. So we went to help, do that, then had a big supper afterwards. That was great. And in those days it was horses and carts, and I used to lead the horse about and give it a bunch of grass to eat. I was only a toddler. Great memories really.
[John Gould 26/11/08]

My mother worked at what they all did then. Buxton was full of visitors. She came from Northampton with her sister, her mother and her brother. They all came here to Buxton. She worked at a hotel up Manchester Road, next to the hospital on the right. It was called the Clarendon. Later on it was a nurses' home for the

Devonshire Hospital. I don't know what it is now. All these people came from away, working here. Even my wife did. She came from Anglesey.

They had a regular orchestra at the Gardens. We used to roller-skate in the Gardens on a Saturday night. I was only young then. Where the Playhouse was there's the Paxton Suite now, but when we were young it was called the Hippodrome, it was a cinema. There used to be a bottling firm in Buxton, it was called R. Lane and Sons, they sold half-pint bottles of stout and beer. And these customers used to throw the bottles away onto heaps and we used to go scrounging for these bottles, find them in these heaps, wash them, clean them and take them to a pub. On Holmfield, at Burbage, there was a pub called the Red Lion. We used to go there and a get a halfpenny each for them. And we used to go to the Hippodrome on a Saturday afternoon for a penny. There was a gallery in there then, it was twopence up there. Years later they took the gallery down.
[Percy Armitt 09/12/08]

Between the two quarries of Dowlow and Hindlow there was a wall. In the days when I was courting you could actually walk along it. In those days we didn't realise the dangers or we wouldn't have gone any-where near it. So we walked along from one end to the other, with a big drop either side. We must have been absolutely crazy, but we were in love. Since then, of course, it's weathered and sections of it have fallen away; the blasting either side's brought it down.
[John Gould 15/11/08]

All these girls came from away, working here. In fact my mother did, she came from Northampton work-ing here at these hotels. This place was full of visitors, you know, the *Advertiser* used to be called *Buxton Advertiser and List of Visitors*. Every hotel put the names of the people who were staying with them. Then they didn't have cars, stay a night and clear off. They used to come by train, used to stop weeks. And the names of the people, 'Mrs and Mrs So-and-So, London' . They all had these servants, like my wife was. My wife came from Anglesey, they were farmers, on a big farm. There were ten of them, she was the youngest. A family at Chapel-en-le-Frith, who owned a holiday home on Anglesey, they used to go to their farm for butter and eggs while they were there. They asked her if she'd like a job at their home and she came work-ing at Chapel-en-le-Frith. She had two cousins doing the same job on Burlington Road and they asked her to try and get somewhere in Buxton and she got a job as a cook general, cooking, cleaning everything. We used to go to Manchester a lot, it used to be half-a-crown return from Buxton to Belle Vue, and we

Percy Armitt and friends at the Cavendish Golf Club, Early 1900s   *Pupils of Sterndale Moor School,* image courtesy of Peter Wardle

used to have a fireworks session on a Saturday night. Later on we used to go to Manchester for our suits, a men's outfitters, and it was called 'Fifty-Bob Shop'. Nothing over fiftybob.
[Percy Armitt 24/11/08]

My name's Frank Ermerson. I live in Buxton now, but originally I came from Manchester. I was born in Preston. We travelled about a bit. My father used to work for local authorities so he travelled about from area to area. We started in Preston, then we moved to Chesterfield, then Manchester. And from there I came down to Buxton in the late-60s and I've been there ever since.

I came here caving and pot-holing when I was a lad and I met a local girl and married her, and that was that really.
[Frank Emerson 10/01/09]

My mother came from Crowdicote, that's near Longnor, Staffordshire, and my father came from New Mills. I grew up in Warslow in Staffordshire. My parents used to have a shop there. I hated it because I had to fill the shelves every night before I could go out anywhere.

(d) Admission of wives of members and daughters over 18.

After a lengthy discussion it was decided that the wives of members and their daughters over 18, should be admitted to the Club buildings on Sunday evening, 30th January, and 13th February, as visitors to the Club.

Separate notices to this effect should be posted in the Club buildings. The next Council Meeting would then be able to review the position and consider whether the experiment had been a success or not, and whether it was worth continuing.

The business of the meeting closed at 9.10.p.m.

Extract from Sterndale Moor Social Club Minutes, 01/02/1938

We used to go for walks a lot because we lived near the Manifold Valley and went for a lot of walks down there. We played lots of games like hopsctotch and jacks, things like that. There were only six girls my age, in the village so it was quite good.

School was all right. I went to an all-girls school in Leek until I was fourteen, then they built a school in Warslow and we had to go to that for the last year. We absolutely hated that because we'd got boys with us then, it wasn't the same. The lessons changed, it was completely different, hardly any cookery lessons, for example. Then I went to the College of Further Education for shorthand-typing.
[Beryl Betts 10/01/09]

The best thing about my childhood was, I think, roaming the countryside. There was no fear and we could just walk about, people didn't lock their doors to their houses and it was the freedom really.

Times were really hard, in actual fact. We never seemed to go on holiday. I think the longest holiday I went on with my parents – we used to go very regularly to Skegness on the Sunday morning, then come back

John Gould, *Sterndale Moor in the snow*, 2008

Sunday evening – on just one occasion we stayed one night. I think that was sum total of my holidays. It was when we were in Sheffield that we did that, just prior to the war. During the war people just did not have holidays. You did whatever you had to do to just survive.
[Brian Young 21/01/09]

These roads before tarmac was invented were terrible, dust and so on. After they'd started making this tarmac it wasn't perfect and sometimes it used to stick to the soles of your shoes. They improved it later on, made it better, but when it was first invented it was terrible. When you walked down the road your shoes would come off!
[Percy Armitt 09/12/08]

I didn't have many ambitions unfortunately, although I now enjoy painting, so maybe a career in art would have been ideal. When I was at school in the 1960s, they didn't exactly push you towards anything else, certainly academic-wise. Basically when you left school you were let off the leash to go to local companies like Ferodo or the quarries. You were expected to do that.

My grandfather was a local farmer. He used to plough with the big shire horses, which was pretty good really. I would love to have seen that. My father worked when he was younger on the farm and then he went into the Army. When he came out of the Army he worked for Ferodo at Chapel until he retired.
[Russell Walker 21/01/09]

My grandparents were farmers on a farm called Burrs Farm at Chelmorton. They had four children, three lads and a girl, and my father worked around the farm a bit. But to supplement that he worked in the quarry. My dad was born in 1895, at the outbreak of the First World War, he was one of the first people to volunteer and he went in the Army. He served four years in Belgium and France. When he came out he started work in the quarries at Blackwell Mill, Tunstead and Cowdale. He eventually came to work at Hindlow. He worked for forty years in total for ICI.
[John Gould 26/11/08]

Looking back on it I thought, at the time, it was sometimes a bit rough but, I really enjoyed it mainly. Being born at Chelmorton, it was mainly a farming area, a little farming village. The people that worked there, to supplement their wages, came up to the quarries here. They walked over the fields, they didn't have a car or a bus or anything like that at that time, they walked to work and walked back home at night. It was quite a different style to what it is now.

When I was at school, and it is 'when I was at school' because I used to snick off quite a bit, bunk off quite a bit, I wanted to be a farmer when I left school, to work on the farms. At night, after finishing school, I used to help out on the farms. I really enjoyed it and I wanted to work with animals, feed the lambs, but my dad had a say; 'Before you try that life, you can do that any time, I'd like you to try a trade first.'

So he went and got me a job as an apprentice at Hodgkinson's garage in Buxton on the Market Place, Scarsdale Place. I worked in there from when I was fifteen to twenty-one, so I served my apprenticeship before going into the Army for two years. Came out, then went back at the garage for twelve months and then went for a walk down the road and got myself a job at the ICI quarry in 1961.
[John Gould 28/10/08]

My name is Kenneth Hibbert and I'm from Buxton, I've spent all my life there. My grandparents worked on the railway because they were in the railway cottages [Blackwell Mill]. My grandfather used to inspect all the tunnels, he went right down to Millers Dale. He enjoyed it. My parents were working in Ferodo, or Duron as it was then, making brake linings for cars. That was a local factory.

Early days I was working in a laundry, driving a laundry van. They've gone now. Then I moved into the quarry and I was there for forty-one years.
[Kenneth Hibbert 21/01/09]

My name is Neville Boam. I was born in the village of Flagg, which is just over the hill from here [Sterndale Moor], about two miles away. That's where I went to school. My parents – my father was born in Taddington, which again is a village just about three miles from where I was born, and my mother originated from about half-way between.

My wife was born and lived in Bakewell, so when we got married we got a house in Bakewell. It wasn't far then from where I worked, which was Dowlow, just down the road from here.

I can remember playing at school, that sort of thing. We didn't go to a very big school, there were only

Rotary Kilns at Tunstead Quarry, c1950s, image courtesy of Tarmac Buxton Lime & Cement

Jim Robinson, *Dowlow Quarry,* 2008

about fifteen or twenty of us all together in the school. We didn't really leave the village. You either went home for your lunch or were taken by taxi to the next village for the school lunches.

What did I want to be? That's a difficult one to answer. It was what I *didn't* want to be. Because my family were farmers, although I had to help out on the farm, I didn't want to do farming, so it was a case of what could I do when I left school?

Unlike today, when I was coming up to leaving school, my father went to the job centre and came back with half a dozen places. I rather fancied some sort of clerical work and my father came back with the applications, one of which was for British Railways as they were called. I applied there and got an interview and I started work in January 1961. I liked it. I worked in the offices and it was dealing with people; selling tickets, sending parcels away and dealing with the general public and I really enjoyed that. I stayed there until 1969. Things were going downhill then on the railways and they were making cutbacks so I decided to change. And the next thing I wanted to do was be a lorry driver.

I got a job with a local haulier and I drove a lorry for twelve months. At the end of twelve months that seemed enough of tearing up and down the country. It was something I wanted to do and I'd done it, it was time for a change.

I was friendly with a lad who worked at Dowlow, he was a joiner then. I asked him if there were any jobs going up there and he said he'd enquire. He came back and said the Manager says come up for an interview, there could be a job there. I went up for an interview and in 1971 I started at Dowlow. And I was there till last Sunday [4th January 2009] when I retired.
[Neville Boam 21/01/09]

My name's Elizabeth Robinson, I live in Sterndale Moor and I work at Lafarge. I've lived here about twenty-one years. I was born and brought up in Fairfield, Buxton. For a short while we lived at Flash, then we moved to Sterndale Moor. My father came from Buxton and my mother came from Dove Holes. When they married they moved to Fairfield.

We had a lot of freedom when I was a child. We played out, hopscotch, drawn on the pavement, skipping, lots of things like that.

I went to school in Fairfield. My school was on the Common, then it moved to Boarstones Lane. I wanted to be a hairdresser; but when I started doing the training I didn't like it. I've never been stuck on any one thing.
[Elizabeth Robinson 21/01/09]

We're both fourteen. We've both lived in this area all our lives. We were both born in Stepping Hill Hospital in Stockport.
[Lucy Robinson and Tom Beresford 15/11/08]

My dad was a farmer, during the war they called it a reserved occupation being a farmer, but he wanted to be a rear-gunner. He applied, but they turned him down for that because he was no good at algebra. A fortnight later they sent him his call-up papers for the Army because they said, 'If you're free to be a rear-gunner you're free to go in the Infantry.' Sent him to India for four years.
[Jim Robinson 10/01/09]

I live in Buxton, I work at Dowlow Quarry and I'm an electrician. I've lived in Buxton all my life. We played football in the winter, sledging and tobogganing. We used to go out all day and freeze to death. Cricket in the summer.
[Peter Betts 10/01/09]

My best childhood memories – now you're asking. It's probably of my grandparents, things we used to do with them, places we used to go with them.

Education was in Buxton, Kents Bank, an all-boys school. Then I went to the College, which was all-boys again. I did a college course in motor engineering and then I went straight to work from the age of fifteen when I left school. I've worked ever since.
[Neil Cocker 21/01/09]

I was born in Chesterfield, in the back bedroom of our house in Chesterfield in the middle of a snowdrift. But that's a complex story!

My grandfather on my mother's side worked for the National Coal Board in the offices. He was an accounts clerk of some sort, I believe. He dealt, I think, with payments of the miners and people who worked in the quarry. My father had a couple of jobs. The last job he worked for the NAAFI, ordering goods that went out to British troops around the world at various Army and Air Force bases and the shops at those places.

My first job was in a horrible, tatty recording studio that was not much bigger than the average bathroom and was above a leather shop. It was the grottiest place you've ever seen and, surprisingly enough, it used to churn out some quite good hits. It was an interesting studio, but I only worked there for a short time. I then went to work in the radio industry, I went to work for one of the very first offshore pirate radio stations on a fort in the Thames Estuary. And that led on to work that I did subsequently. It was interesting, it was the first of several stations that I worked on. I got sacked for not playing a Frank Sinatra record.

My early education was pretty boring, I suppose. I was always in dispute with the schools inasmuch as I felt that they crammed – well, they didn't cram, they tended to spread over three terms something they could easily do in one term. I got totally bored, quite honestly. I suppose that what I tended to do, I learned more reading books on the back of a bus going to and from school than I learned at school.

I never planned to go into the career that I went into. I wanted to be an architect, I trained to be an architect. I was actually rather good at technical drawing. I discovered I could do technical drawing well so I planned on becoming an architect. But I never did it because I heard a record once that I liked, a rather unusual record. I couldn't analyse how it had been recorded, couldn't figure it out, couldn't work out what instruments were on it, so I set out to find the person who'd recorded it. It took me six months to find him and, when I did find him, that eventually led to the job I got in the studio.
[Printz Holman 03/12/08]

Daniel Astill, *Club sign by the A515*, 2009

Heading Crew at Cowdale Quarry, image courtesy of Tarmac Buxton Lime & Cement

Hand charging a shot hole, 1931, image courtesy of Tarmac Buxton Lime & Cement

Sterndale Moor Gardens Association - Hon. Secretary, Mr. H.S. Eyre. It was agreed that it was an excellent show, £10. was realised for the Red Cross Agriculture Fund.

Club Robbery 16th August. 44-64.

The Secretary reported on the Club robbery of August 16th and stated that the Steward in his report on the occurrence estimated that approximately £23. 10. 7. had been stolen, which amount included the cost of cigarettes stolen, £1. 17. 6. Football Club subscription money and 19/4d Steward's dinner money. Of the amount of cash stolen, £21. 0. 0. had been recovered. The Secretary and Treasurer were requested to submit their recommendations for the disposal of the £21. 0. 0. at the next meeting.

14 ft. Leather Upholstered Seat. 44-65.

It was reported that a 14 ft. leather upholstered seat had been delivered to the Club on Wednesday, 9th August, from Royal Exchange on the instructions of Mr. G.W. Garlick, Estate Manager. This was much appreciated. The Secretary was asked to obtain a supply of bolts so that the Steward might repair the Club's chairs.

Club Verandah 'Black-out' Partition. 44-66.

It was reported that the Steward, on the Estate Manager's authority, had removed the 'black-out' partition on the Club verandah.

It was agreed Mr. S. Barlow be asked to write to the Police for permission to use the outside light on the corner of the Club.

Supplies - Rum and Wine. 44-67.

The Secretary reported on a communication received from Messrs. Marston, Thompson and Evershed Limited, explaining the basis on which present quotas of Rum and Wine were supplied. The Secretary also stated that the Steward had requested permission to approach Messrs. Ormes and Co. Ltd., Bakewell, for supplies of Wines, Spirits, Bottled Beer and Guinness, etc. This was granted.

It was agreed, in view of the reduction in supplies, that a trial rationing of Bottled Beer and Guinness be carried out, and the Secretary was asked to arrange that 1/36th month's delivery be sold over the counter each Monday to Friday, and 2/36th each Saturday and Sunday

Christmas Handicaps Finals. 44-68.

It was agreed to hold the Christmas Handicaps Finals on the 21st or 23rd December, subject to one of these dates being convenient for Major L.G. Sewell, whom it was unanimously agreed be invited to present the prizes.

Extract from Sterndale Moor Social Club Minutes, 08/11/1944

Sterndale Moor and the Social Club

June 1937 they opened the club. I'm not sure whether the school opened at the same time. I spoke to somebody called Joan Barson, she was Joan Riley when she lived up here. She could remember starting in 1938, so I could imagine the school did open at the same time, and I'm not sure how you'd check it. So many people that I've spoken to can't remember anything about it at all. Then other people, like Doris Wardle who used to live up here, could remember everything, but isn't with us any more.

When it opened there were sixty to seventy pupils went to it, so that's quite a lot. The function room that they have the dances in, there was a partition in the middle of the room, so it made two rooms; one room they had two classes in and I think they were the primary-school children, and the other room they had for the older pupils. They had a school canteen, but that didn't open straight away. Mrs Riley, from up here, she was the cook and Mrs Jones, who used to live on the front along here, she was the assistant cook and I believe made fantastic meals. Then Doris Wardle used to help out as well. So I don't think there'd be a lot of space with sixty or seventy children in.

But it was a good school. I think the teachers were very good. There was a Miss Tesh, she was the Headmistress. Mary Wilton, she taught at school, and a Sally Robinson, but that name doesn't mean a thing to me. Later, when Miss Tesh left, there was a Miss Healey came. I don't know how long she was at the school. I think she came from Hartington way.

The children came from Pomeroy and, and at one time, on the works, people used to live up there, there were quite a lot of houses up there. They used to come down to the school. And the children came from the surrounding farms. I didn't ever go to the school. I came up here in 1950 and that was the year I started at Cavendish Grammar School in Buxton.
[Jean Gould 01/02/09]

Places like this, that were built by ICI specifically for the workers, this club was built in 1937 specifically for the ICI employees to start with. No ladies in to start with either, but that came in pretty quick after. Everyone knew everybody in the village, whether it was a good thing or a bad thing… People talked to each other a lot, played games, indoor and outdoor games; football, cricket, tug of war, chess, all the table games, darts, dominoes, snooker, billiards. It was nice to come to. A lot of competition going on. It really stimulated a lot of camaraderie.

Tegwyn Holman, *View of Dowlow Quarry from the village* , 2008

Daniel Astill, *View from the club,* 2008

There were several shops in this village. Where I live was a little shop and there was one somewhere down here in the bottom. There were three shops all together. Plus, at the beginning of the village, as you come up the A515 from Buxton, there was a Co-operative store built, where they brought all the provisions. A chap from there would come round on a certain day and take your order for the next week and it would be delivered by van from that store there.

It closed down because it became non-viable, really. When the big superstores opened up in Buxton, they had everything that the Co-op had. So it's just the old story, they were cheaper and the Co-op couldn't stock a big variety of stuff. One shop would perhaps have a few things, another different stuff, another a few cigarettes, that's how it worked.
[John Gould 15/11/08]

Over the years ICI gradually let the houses go and people like myself have now bought the houses. They're now privately owned, none are owned by ICI. There's been an influx of people who don't work in the quarries. There aren't as many quarry jobs going now because it used to be manual and it's not now. So that's been a big change. People have improved their houses and built on, and it's looking good. The village is getting quite established now.

We still, of course, have people in the village who work in the quarries. We're still very dependent on the quarries because they're a huge source of income for people and it puts money into the community. The quarry has been a mainstay of the community for many years, and still is.
[John Gould 26/11/08]

I think one of the most interesting stories about snow in Sterndale Moor was in the winter of 1947. I don't remember this, I wasn't here at the time, but it's a story that has been passed down. There is a railway line behind me that goes up to the quarries, it actually goes up to the quarry at the top and finishes. But at one time that was a line that went on to Cromford and to Ashbourne. And in 1947 there was a very, very heavy snowfall, in fact there were snowdrifts that were six foot, seven foot, eight foot plus and on the line almost immediately opposite this club, one of the trains came up and got stuck in the snow. It actually became almost totally buried under a snowdrift. The locomotive had to be abandoned, it couldn't go on, and it was there several weeks, I understand.

When they eventually got a snow plough from Buxton out to it – the snow plough is actually put on to the front of another steam locomotive to push the snow out of the way – they got out to the locomotive here and they brought a crew out. You can't just start the steam locomotive like you can a car, can't just turn the ignition key. You have to clean it all out, put wood in, you have to light a fire and put coal on it. They'd brought some wood with them to light the fire and they put the wood in. Then they turned to the tender to put the coal on the fire, knowing that a steam locomotive comes on its journey with a whole load of coal on it, and the tender was absolutely empty.

You can understand that at this time houses over here were all heated by coal. The coal-man used to come once a week and he hadn't been for several weeks, but when they looked across at Sterndale Moor all the chimneys were smoking merrily away.
[Printz Holman 03/12/08]

Dowlow Quarry, January 1939,
image courtesy of Lafarge Aggregates

I remember in '47 we tried to get a train through from Higher Buxton Station. We got through to Hindlow Station and there's a gully before you get to ICI Hindlow and Dowlow and it got stuck in there. Couldn't go any further. All the electricity was overhead. They had us quarrymen breaking ice, going round with these poles knocking ice off. And we had a gang of men walking to Brierlow Bar; vans and whatever could get to Brierlow Bar, but they couldn't get up the hill to get to Sterndale Moor. They were bringing food. All Sterndale Moor residents were ICI people, ICI built those houses. The gang of men carried food up for these people because they couldn't work in the quarries.
[Percy Armitt 24/11/08]

A lot went on in the club, or the school, when I was younger. We used to have St John Ambulance and most of the children who lived up here took part in it. Mr Harrison ran it, he was also the first-aid person on the works. And Mrs Tomlinson, who was a councillor, she was part of it. We used to have a very good team that went all over the place doing competitions and we did win quite a few cups and things when we were all together. We also trained, and I know this sounds silly, we also trained the police in Buxton. They took it up and they used to come up here for their training. There were quite a lot of us. We went to Doncaster and we were reviewed by Princess Margaret and we thought that was great.

We had a fantastic youth club, it all took place in the function room, you weren't allowed in the other side where the snooker tables are, children just weren't allowed in there then. So we all used to be in the function room and we had the youth club and we put quite a few concerts on, the stage was there still. We used to have quite a nice time really. At one time there was something to do nearly every night up here.

We weren't allowed in the club, in fact when I first came up here, we weren't allowed in the school-yard. The man who was running it then, Mr Tenniswood, Bill Tenniswood, frightened everybody to death. He lived opposite the school, the club, and if he saw anybody in or anybody dropping anything, litter or anything, he went ballistic and you were frightened to death of him. So it was completely different to what it is now.
[Jean Gould 01/02/09]

It goes round and round really. When we first came to live here probably 70 per cent of the people that lived up here did actually work in one of the quarries. Now there's hardly anybody who actually works in the quarry. The place itself kind of revolves around the club, but the club over the years has changed as well and does different things. And I think, like I said to you earlier, my friend who lives over the way was born and brought up here and she went to school in the club. Like when the 'cowboys' came [the club is home to 'Rebels Retreat', formerly known as 'High Peak Country and Western Club']. It was on the verge of shutting down and then they started using it and they've picked it up. And it does that, the club goes down to rock bottom, then picks up again.

I can't imagine Sterndale Moor without the club. To be honest, I think it would kill a lot of the community, the spirit. We probably only come to the club every other week, we make a point of coming down, having a drink and meeting with friends. But I can go in that fortnight that I haven't been in, I might not see anyone, only my immediate neighbour, like John. People are busy working, out in the day, so yes, it would be a big deal if anything happened to it.

I think we've been lucky to bring our kids up in a place like this because in other places they couldn't have the freedom that they have here; able to go over to the park. I've got friends who live in town and it's a big deal just to take your kids to the park for an hour, whereas we can let them go. They can wander about. They camp in this field, in summer, in all weather, and things like that. You couldn't let them do that in other places.
[Elizabeth Robinson 29/01/09]

Then it got down that there were only about ten children left at the school and it wasn't really viable and they decided to close the school and for everybody to go to Harpur Hill, and that's what they did. The kids used the school bus to go to Harpur Hill.

ICI used to run the club, then the members took over and started running it.
[Jean Gould 01/02/09]

Marriage brought me to Sterndale Moor. I was born in a city, lived in town all my life, and it was basically a cheap place to live and start my family off. I've lived here twenty-three years this year.

All I do is work, and now and again I come into the club. It's very important. It's a focal point of the village and I think a lot more people should get involved with it. I've been involved with the club for twenty-two of the twenty-three years I've been up here. There's 'cowboys' come, Country and Western, nearly every weekend. We have an annual bonfire night and various village fetes. Stuff like that. It's quite entertaining.

I worked on the bar for eighteen years. It's like one big family really. You get to know everybody. Everybody you see, every time they come in. If you leave a conversation one night, the next night you can carry it on. It's very good.
[Neil Cocker 21/01/09]

I moved to Sterndale Moor in 1987. I actually had been working in London for quite a while because that's where the radio industry is based and it's where most of my work was. Basically, as technology started changing, I was in a situation where I could live anywhere in the world – well, anywhere sunny, anyway. It may seem surprising that I chose Sterndale Moor as the place I wanted to live. I had a sort of criteria: I wanted to live in Derbyshire again, having been born here and having lived in Derbyshire for chunks of my life; I wanted to live close to the Peak National Park, but I didn't want to live in it. If you look at the map the Peak Park actually goes right round Sterndale Moor, it follows the main road, goes round it and goes on the road again. It sort of fitted my criteria.
[Printz Holman 03/12/08]

We've just had a bonfire night and the whole village comes down to watch all the fireworks and then comes and has tea here. Everyone's here and all the little kids are here. If the club wasn't here we couldn't do anything like that.
[Lucy Robinson 15/11/08]

There's quite an interesting football match which is held sometimes up here, has been held on fundraising things, where we challenge our local teams which you draw together. We've always won it simply because we know where the holes are in the pitch.
[Printz Holman 03/12/08]

I want to live here when I'm older, with my family. It's a nice place to live. It's a friendly atmosphere here and it's like, my friends that live in Buxton, it's completely different. Even though it's a bigger place the families feel like … there's clubs everywhere and at kicking-out time you're worried that something's going to happen to them, so their parents don't trust them as much. There's not much that really can happen here. We've got more freedom, definitely. My mum always says if I'm in Buxton for the evening I have to be home for a certain time, but if I'm here, as long as I'm in the club and she knows where I am, then it's all right.
[Lucy Robinson 15/11/08]

Kerra Holman, *View from my window,* 2009

TOM: When the 'cowboys' come up we join in with their activities outside. We do shooting.

LUCY: And we camp outside a lot in the summer.

TOM: The 'cowboys' is a group, they come up every Saturday and dance and stuff. And there's a live artist and they do fake gun-fighting. And sometimes they have long weekends at Bank Holidays and we do archery and knife throwing and axe throwing.

LUCY: When they come up it gives us something to do over the weekend. And we do get involved. And we get awards and certificates for doing it. They're very friendly and nice. We know some of the songs. We know some of the dances.

TOM: They're not that bad the songs.

LUCY: There's some songs that we know, like the rock-and-roll type, but they've really settled into the club now.

TOM: They come every week, so we've just got used to them.

LUCY: They're like locals now.

TOM: We all have our nicknames. I'm called Tom Horn because there was a gunfighter called Tom Horn.

LUCY: I'm called Desert Rose because of the song.

TOM: There's Preacher, he's the DJ and is really loud. There's Miss Maverick, who's my sister.

LUCY: My sister's called Shortfire. Darkwolf comes up every Bank Holiday and he's like the best shooter. He wins quite a lot. There's Wrangler and he's got a gang but, they're from another place in the country so they only come up about once a month. Then there's groupies from the band, usually.

TOM: My friends don't know what happens here.

LUCY: My friends know and they don't really care. They just think it's one of those things. They all have different clubs. They go to youth clubs on Friday and we can't. This is like our youth club. They understand. They've been here before and watched us dancing and shooting. They think we're a bit weird, but it's like… It's fun. We enjoy doing it.

[Lucy Robinson and Tom Beresford 15/11/08]

Charity football match at the club, image courtesy of Peter Wardle

There were quarries at Harpur Hill, Hillhead Quarries at Harpur Hill, the next one was Ryan and Somerville at Hindlow and over the road at Hindlow, there's another quarry there. It was Beswick's, but it's another name now. Hoffman Quarry at Harpur Hill. Farther over was ICI Hindlow, where I worked for twenty years, next door is Dowlow Quarries, then down Ashwood Dale was Topley Pike Quarries, higher up was ICI Cowdale Quarries, and opposite was a private quarry, I don't remember the name of that one. Then there was Waterswallows Quarry, Tarmac, ICI at Tunstead, and one at Dove Holes. There's Taylor Frith at Bibbingtons. I counted about thirteen. There's about three now, the others all shut.

All around Buxton there were quarries at the side of the road that were used by farmers, I think. The Punch Bowl, that caravan site up Manchester Road, that's a quarry, isn't it? There's one up between Burbage and Ladmanlow, on your left, where those houses are being built, that was a quarry. There's another up the Cat and Fiddle Road, from Ladmanlow going up to Leek and Macc, there's one up there on your left. There's one at Harpur Hill where there's a lot of houses built in front of it. They're all over the place, these quarries.
[Percy Armitt 24/11/08]

When the war was on the Germans dropped fire bombs in a line. It was in the night and when we went to work the next morning, all through the quarry were these fire bombs that had gone off, all along the quarry floor, over the top of the quarry face and down into Earl Sterndale, and it set the church on fire. They managed that. They dropped all these flares through the quarry where we worked. Why did they do it, though? Why in the quarry? I reckon they thought they were over some ammunitions place. There was this ammunitions dump at Harpur Hill. They built a tunnel there and put all the explosives in. Afterwards it was a mushroom factory.

The First World War, all these kilns were open-topped and you could see all the fire from ground level, but after that they built these cupolas. I don't know if they saw some light from Hindlow kilns and tried to drop it on that and missed it.

There were three quarries at Hindlow. One was called the 'hold', where I worked, the next one was the 'middle lift', lower down, then right down where the chimneys are now was the 'lump stone hold'. Six-inch

The beginning of Tunstead Quarry, 1929, image courtesy of Tarmac Buxton Lime & Cement

stone there, a 'Brunner'. We would load wagons for Brunner Mond [later merged with three other chemical companies to form Imperial Chemical Industries (ICI)], they called it 'Brunner stone'. Six-inch stone, nothing over six-inch, and it was taken over to Northwich. They bought it off Buxton Lime. In fact, when I was working at Hindlow, they'd come round and say, 'Will you fill us a Brunner wagon.' You got paid more for breaking it small.

When the war was on, I don't know how long it lasted, but they brought a coachload of businessmen from Manchester, filling on the Sunday, when we weren't at work. Every man had their own wagon there to fill. But these businessmen made a mess of it and when we went on a Monday morning we had to clear up after them. They picked all the handy stone, whatever there was; we called them 'muckers'.

None of us went in the Army, we were in a Reserved Occupation, all the fillers in the quarry. You can't make a lot of things in this country without lime, and one of the main things is steel, you can't make steel without lime. They used a lot of steel in the war.
[Percy Armitt 28/01/09]

There was a sense of community amongst the workforce. In a job like that, it's like mining. You were relying on your friends for your safety. Someone might see something you hadn't seen and they'd tell you. If there's a bad stone on the quarry face, yes, you worked as a team and you looked after one another.
[Kenneth Hibbert 21/01/09]

Another thing, up to 1942, we used to go to work and we didn't work in the wet; if it was raining, we used to stay in the cabins, you didn't go out because it wasn't safe. When I worked in the quarries I saw five people killed. Four of them, workmen in a quarry, they were stone-fillers, they were 'getters'. A 'getter' was a man who got the stone down, who blasted in bulk. Then there was a 'popper'. When they fired these blasts, a lot of the stone was big, you know, impossible to break with a hammer. They had people with a pneumatic drill, drilling in and then putting a cartridge with a fuse on it, and they had firing times in the quarry: half-past eight, ten o'clock, twelve o'clock, two o'clock and four o'clock. They had five firing times in the day at the quarry and they fired these stones up to make them smaller. Even then you had to break them down. You hadn't to put anything in these wagons over forty pounds, which is a stone about ten or twelve inches long and about five inches deep. No bigger than that otherwise, when it went for lime burning, the fire wouldn't burn through the stone and it would leave a core inside of stone. That was no good to people who wanted pure lime.
[Percy Armitt 24/11/08]

Cora Glasser, *Cement Plant at Tunstead Quarry*, 2008

Dowlow Lime Works, image courtesy of Lafarge Aggregates

My first job was in a chemical factory, which was Seldon Research down the Ashbourne Road from here. I was there for five years, then I went to Duron, which was a brake manufacturer. I was there for two years and from there I went to Tunstead Quarry for a further five years and then from there up to Hindlow.
[**Neil Cocker 21/01/09**]

At Hindlow we used to have an order and they called it china stone, that's stone pure with no markings on it. We used to put it on one side until we'd got a tub full and load it up and we got extra for it. Half-a-crown a wagon for it. China stone – it went for making face powder, stuff like that.
[**Percy Armitt 24/11/08**]

There was a strong sense of community, especially where I worked. Dowlow Quarry started in 1899 when it was a private company being run by three or four different families, and it stayed like that until 1969 when it was bought by a company called Steetley, who at that time were based in Worksop in Nottinghamshire. The Chairman was associated with the steel industry in Sheffield, so they bought Dowlow and put some lime kilns on it to supply the steel industry in Sheffield with burnt lime.

Then in 1992 that firm was taken over by another company called Redland, who were big road-stone and building trade suppliers. The steel industry by then had declined and Steetley had closed the kilns down because there was not enough demand for the materials.

In 1999 Redland were taken over by a company called Lafarge, who are the owners now. They are, I believe, the world's biggest aggregate producer, not only aggregates now because they've purchased Blue Circle Cement, so they're one of the world's biggest cement producers. After they'd taken over Dowlow they realised the section that I worked for, which produces the finer materials, wasn't in keeping with their main industry so they sold it off to Omya, who own it now. Omya do the industrial minerals material and Lafarge do the road-stone, tarmac and building trade. So that's the history of Dowlow, it's been there 110 years.
[**Neville Boam 21/01/09**]

There was definitely a sense of community. There was a greater sense of community at Hindlow than Tunstead, because at Tunstead it was more as though the people came from a town, if you understand what I'm trying to say. They came and did a job. Whereas at Hindlow a lot of the people where what they called

'Wheelbarrow Farmers'. That was people who had a small-holding, but it was not sufficient to feed a family, so they came out to work here and they also looked after a small-holding at home. In other words, they were more like country folk. They were very loyal people. They'd always turn out if you wanted something doing or something went wrong. They'd always come to work in the snow, in the winter, whatever.
[**Brian Young 21/01/09**]

Going back to the times between the two wars, things were pretty hard and it was very difficult finding a job and people would go to quite great lengths to find one. I heard the story of Fred Shaw, who used to live in one of the houses on the front [Sterndale Moor]. There are several variations of the story, I think people put their own spin on it, but the way Fred told it to me was that he came from somewhere over Stockport way and he set out to find a job. He walked in an easterly direction and stopped at a lot of companies along the way, knocking at doors asking if they'd got a job. He ended up at the quarry just opposite here, asked them if they'd got a job, they offered him one and he eventually came to live in the house at number 12 Sterndale Moor. At that time he had the job as a teenager, and he spent his entire working life over at the quarry. He eventually retired and he passed away a few years ago.
[**Printz Holman 03/12/08**]

In those days, it was hard manual labour in the main. I mean, you had the people in the offices who paid your wages and looked after the time-sheets, one thing and another. There used to be up to 400 people working in this quarry, loading stone in Jubilees by hand and breaking this huge stone into smaller lumps with a hammer. It was physical hard work and cold, and you didn't have, in those days, the equipment, protective clothing, that you have now. You had to provide your own. It was a real hard job. My father worked up here for about thirty years and it was rough going at times. And you didn't get paid if you were off, at that time. It was just hard work and if you weren't there, you didn't get paid.
[**John Gould 15/11/08**]

When I first went up, in '38, ICI brought some good things out. They started giving paid holidays. They had a long-service award: a silver watch for twenty years and a gold watch for thirty, I got those; a clock for forty years and I did thirty-nine and a half, so I didn't get a clock!

There were five kilns and four of us were 'getters', a very dangerous job, you know. You drilled these holes and put powder in for a big blast. I always remember, it was one afternoon, and he [a 'getter'] bored these

powder holes on the top of the quarry. He was in a shelter with a plunger, a charger that would explode the flash, and when the hooter went to fire these chargers, he turned the hammer and the wire that went to the explosives in this powder hole. There must have been a wind or something, and it blew this wire onto some electric cables on the road behind him and electrocuted him. He lived at Longnor. There aren't many left who filled stone. We stopped hand-filling at Hindlow in '56 when I left there.
[Percy Armitt 24/11/08]

'Chatter' is where you get a lot of dirt. There's another gang of men, you call them 'bearers'. On top of the quarry is perhaps a foot, or a couple of foot, of earth before you get to the bare stone. Instead of blowing the soil amongst all the stone, they had these bearers cleaning this soil off and taking it away. Then when it was fired it was all stone. But even then there were bits of parts of clay and stuff. When you'd broken this stone by hand, you either filled what they called 'mucker' with the soil, clean it up, or, if it's all stone, 'chatter'. You can sell that, but mucker they used to take onto a tip, refuse tip. Chatter, they had an order for that, making roads and things like that.

Dad retired about 1931, something like that. He'd been working there as long as I could remember. Dad didn't talk about working in the quarries much. There wasn't much safety about it. At Hindlow they had five firing periods in a day where you lit all your fuses to break all these stones up. You ran to a shelter while they went off. At Grin Quarry they had no shelters. If someone was firing, letting some blasts off, they'd walk to the edge and shout, 'Keep your heads up.' They wouldn't allow it now.

At ICI Hindlow they had concrete igloos. They made these igloos while I was working there. Before that they had wooden shelters made from railway sleepers. It was dangerous.

When I was working here on Grin, on the kilns, I finished work about four o'clock and I didn't live far away. I was walking along this field, going home, and there was a blast went off in the quarry about half a mile away. I heard a warning sound. I looked up and there was a stone, about that, coming through the air and making a noise, a hell of a noise, and I stopped and it dropped in front of me and buried itself in the ground. If you put too much powder in, it'll throw a stone a hell of a way.

That's why I say a 'getter's' job – they brought the stone down – was a responsible job. They'd put too much powder in or not enough. It's a job I wouldn't have wanted. I saw four getters killed, one filler and a popper.

The hooter used to go three times, a couple of minutes before firing time, then it'd go twice to get ready to light your fuses, then perhaps a minute after that there'd be a long, one hooter and that's when you lit and ran back into the shelter. The fuses were about eighteen inches long. But a fuse, you can light it with a match, but perhaps you'd have half a dozen fuses wanting lighting and you couldn't do that, keep lighting matches. You know sparkler fireworks – they had one of them and you could light that and go round all the fuses and it set them all off. You couldn't do it with matches, how long would it take you? That was at Hindlow. That gave you time to run to the shelter about thirty yards away.

There were some women working at the quarry. At other quarries women had made the igloos, but that didn't happen where I worked.

I remember one woman from Chelmorton who worked on the locos. The locos would come round here and they'd have a 'waggoner', usually a young lad, but this one was a woman. She'd unhook empty wagons, they were in threes running off the main line. They'd have men working there, one for each empty. The loco used to push the loads that were in front of it, push them to the weigh-box and onto the kiln-sidings. It pushed the full ones out and brought the empty ones behind it and the wagoner unhooked the empties to fill again.
[Percy Armitt 09/12/08]

When I left Grin I'd been burning and picking at the kilns at Grin for a while, but when I went to Hindlow work started picking up then just before the war. When I worked at Hindlow, when I first started in '38, I push-biked from Burbage to Hindlow, six miles

Kerra Holman, *View of Tunstead Quarry from Old Moor Quarry*, 2008 57

each way before I started a day's work. I push-biked it for ten years. After that I packed it up and started going down on the bike to Buxton and leaving it with a relative of mine on London Road, and I went on the bus.
[Percy Armitt 24/11/08]

When they had these top holes, they used to bore in from the top, but when you'd moved all that loose stone you got what you called the 'stumps'. It was all solid down here, they were no clay bed. When all the stone had been filled that had come from this top hole, all the bottom was solid. You had to move forward, so they had to bore, these 'poppers' did, all around, in front of you, this stone that was solid, blow it out, and you had to make a floor so that you could move forward, level. If you got in the stumps you worked a damn sight harder for less money, you couldn't fill as many wagons as if it was all loose.
[Percy Armitt 09/12/08]

I used to work at Beswick's Lime Works at Hindlow, it's now owned by Lhoist, I worked there as a short-hand-typist. I was there about seven years. I didn't like making the coffee because I never made it right, some liked it strong and others wanted it weak. I enjoyed typing letters and reports.

It was a small quarry and we all got on. The quarry workers would come down and see us, and we helped them and they helped us. It was great. You've got good and bad wherever you go, but I found them fine.

I could have gone to work at the Halifax Building Society, but I fancied the work in the quarry offices. And, also, when I was at college, training, Beswick's gave me the chance to go and work there in the holidays, which was great, it gave me a good insight into it.
[Beryl Betts 10/01/09]

My first job, I tried to join the Navy when I was sixteen. I left school without telling my parent's which took a little bit of getting over, but we'll not go into that. I went to the DP Battery in Bakewell until they'd let me into the Navy about nine months later.

When I came out I did one or two things on my own and then I joined ICI and worked for them for thirty-four years. Then I took early-retirement at fifty-seven and I've been retired ever since, which is now my twenty-fifth year.

I worked at Tunstead for a while, that's the larger of the two quarries in Buxton. Then I came up to Hindlow

Tegwyn Holman, *View of Tunstead Quarry from the crusher*, 2008

Lucy Robinson, *View of Hindlow Quarry from the Maerz Kiln*, 2008

as the Assistant Manager and then, later on, I was made the Manager of Hindlow, which had the quarry and the kilns, the lime-burning plant and, at one time, the stone-grinding plant. That was quite interesting. **[Brian Young 21/01/09]**

I had various jobs, but it was basically money that brought me to the quarry. I worked for a short time at RMC quarry first, then I moved to Dowlow because it was simply better paid, although RMC now pays more than Dowlow.

Some of my friends work in a similar type of business. Living in this sort of area, that's all the work there is. Ferodo, Otters and quarrying are the main employers. Some of my friends have got their own businesses, some work in offices, but everybody treats you just the same.

The work I'm doing now involves a washing plant that's relatively new, only about five years old. Basically what it does, it takes stone that we used to almost give away, the rubbish end of the stone if you like, so a lot of dirt in it. It got to the stage where we couldn't even give it away; we were just stockpiling millions of tons of it. So they decided to build a washing plant, which does a very good job. It takes the stone, washes it and produces some really good-quality stones, which we now sell. So it's a kind of recycling, in a way.

Conditions in the quarry are not too bad. The safety aspect's got very, very high. It can be dirty, in summer it's incredibly dusty. In fact, in Sterndale Moor on a windy day, people sometimes complain about the dust blowing across their washing. In winter, it's a mud bath. So it can be dirty underfoot, but that's just the nature of the job.

Whilst you're at work there's a sense of community, but outside of work not so much, simply because people come from different areas. Some people come from Buxton, other people come from Sterndale Moor and the villages around, so you don't tend to see many people outside of work.

There have been quite a lot of changes, especially over the last hundred years, from breaking rock by hand, which is incredibly hard work and that's when men were men and they worked in all weathers. Now you've got from fourty-ton dumpers right up to, in the bigger quarries, 100-ton dumpers and that's the amount they actually carry, so that, plus the dumper, you could be talking 150-tons trundling along the quarry roads.

The first job in the quarry I had was the same first job most people had at that time, spare man. You went through every process of the quarry learning each and every job so that you could stand in for any person that was off sick or off on holiday. So you could do every job on site.

Then I progressed to the quarry itself, which was driving dumpers and shovels. It's every kid's dream, I suppose, to drive a big dumper. It's great fun at first, the first week or so. It's interesting because you're in such a big vehicle and at the face-shovel you've got a twelve-ton bucket on the front of your shovel and you're loading the dumpers. It's quite an interesting job because you've got the safety factor of it, you actually get danger money being at the face, because the face can fall down on top of a shovel, so you've got to be constantly aware of things happening around you as you're loading.

The quarry face is the most dangerous place in the quarry. Again, you try and make it as safe as possible. Unfortunately a friend of mine was killed a few years ago. So they've actually cut the face down, they're not as high now and if they do fall, you don't have the same danger. Other than that, the places I work and where most people work, in the yard and on the plant, are pretty safe now. The firm has really become a safe place, as safe as possible anyway.
[Russell Walker 21/01/09]

I went down to Tunstead about three years ago. I hadn't been there for thirty-three years. I was sixteen years there, eighteen at Hindlow and six or seven years here [Grin]. I was about twenty-four when I started. In the thirties it was terrible, there was no work. I was on the dole for six months at a time. Everybody went and signed on every day in the morning. You used to draw your money, about seven shillings a week, on a Friday.
[Percy Armitt 24/11/08]

We used to start at seven finish at four but in wintertime it's dark at seven. You can't work in a quarry in the dark. So six weeks before Christmas and six weeks after we started at eight. When it was daylight. Finished at four but we had to go on the Saturday morning to make up that hour. We lost an hour a day, but we had to go on a Saturday morning to make it up.

We didn't work Christmas Day. Tunstead never stopped, Tunstead kilns, Saturday or Sunday nights, they were going all the time. But they didn't work on Christmas Day, that was the only day.

There was a nickname for the men who would work too hard to earn more money, 'Panzers'. There were three or four who killed themselves up there [by working too hard].

Years ago, everybody up where we lived, they all had nicknames; Butty Bent, Kick-me Nadin, Corky Nadin, Smash Brindley, Gravy Goodwin, Spare 'um Goodwin!
[Percy Armitt 28/01/09]

I was a bit awe-struck when I first went to the quarry, to be honest, because I started as a mechanic at Tunstead Quarry. I'd never seen machines the size of the face-shovel, the diggers and the vehicles. I'd never worked on anything quite that big before; even in the Army I'd worked with some heavy machinery, but nothing like that. I wondered what the hell I'd got myself into, to be honest, to start with. But pretty soon I settled down and for the thirty-odd years I worked in the quarry industry I thoroughly enjoyed it. I always liked going to work.

There used to be hundreds of people involved in the quarry. Now they produce vast amounts of stone with about a tenth of the manpower. That's the big change.
[John Gould 28/10/08]

The kilns worked twenty-four hours a day, they never stopped, every day, three shifts. I never, ever had Saturday and Sunday off the last fifteen years, only at holiday time.

When you were picking lime at the picking belt, both here and at Tunstead, you used to have to have something over your mouth. Stop breathing it in because it'd burn you. I read something about crumbling limestone. Well, there's no limestone

Tom Beresford, *Dowlow Quarry entrance on the A515,* 2008

that crumbles. Look at these stone walls, been here centuries. Limestone doesn't crumble, only when it's been burnt into lime.
[Percy Armitt 28/01/09]

My favourite part was the people because that makes any job, the people you work with. You've got to be happy and enjoy the people you work with. As long as that fits in, the rest will follow naturally. I've enjoyed all the jobs I've ever done, I've enjoyed the people that I've worked with, got on with most of them fairly well, so that's made the job. But I do like planning and organising things and it's fulfilling when they actually work and come to fruition. You feel you've achieved something when it actually happens.

The least favourite was the times we had redundancies and that sort of thing, and people lost their jobs. It was always very sad and it had to happen, and you had to be involved in choosing the people that left. It wasn't very nice having to say goodbye to people you knew were good workers and good friends, if you like. But it's just a fact of industry that is happening today, as you're well aware from all the news stories.

But we definitely need the big holes in the grounds, whether they're there or not. From your point of view, the places like Dowlow supply material to the glass industry, the ceramics industry, animal feeds, human feed, things like 'Shake 'n' Vac' that goes on your carpet, carpet backing, plastics, covering for electric wires, fibre glass, rubber. It goes into all that sort of material, so if you didn't have those places you certainly wouldn't have the type of lifestyle you're living today. If you go home tonight and take everything out of your house that hasn't had some involvement with a hole in the ground, all you'd be left with is the wood. Even the tiles on the roof, the slates, are man-made. All the stones are mainly man-made. Anything to do with steel, the tiles on the floors, the baths, the shower trays, they all contain some form of limestone that have come out of the ground.
[Neville Boam 21/01/09]

I started work at the quarry because it was just convenient. After I'd had my children I wanted a small job, so first of all I worked in a pub, in the Plough in Flagg. Then I heard about the job in the quarry and, because it was only across the road, it was very handy for me. I applied for that and got it.

It's dirty, we have to wear special clothing, which is a bit bulky. It's not bad, the people are nice. I can't think of anyone I don't like and it's a nice atmosphere. I'm a cleaner and I have to clean the canteen and the mess rooms where the men meet, and the toilets and some offices and such like.

Hidden cave revealed after blasting at Hindlow Quarry, 1987, image courtesy of Tarmac Buxton Lime & Cement

They are very good at team work, people work together and not because they're pushed. We're not on extortionate wages or anything like that but, people do tend to stick. I've worked there for almost ten years and I'm kind of like a newcomer in a way. A lot of it's about how the economics are, so sometimes somebody will retire or leave and they aren't replaced. But unless they've retired there's very few that actually leave because they don't like it. Certainly, from my point of view, it is quite a dirty job and sometimes I think, 'What am I doing here?' But there's other things that keep you there, like the men and women I work with; it is just that nice thing that perhaps you wouldn't get if you worked in a supermarket.
[Elizabeth Robinson 29/01/09]

There was nothing else but the quarries round here. When you went signing on they used to ask you where you'd been for a job. I'll tell you what we used to do. We used to go and sign on in the morning and go straight to the Cavendish caddying. They used to come up and try to catch us. They shut this place, it used to be called Burbage Ladies' Golf Club, men played on it too. They closed it in 1926 when they opened Cavendish, there was an eighteen-hole at Cavendish.
[Percy Armitt 24/11/08]

You don't really notice the quarries much. My mum and dad both work in them. I ask my dad what he's done at work and he talks about it. They've all got nicknames and they all have radios. Even if you're on your own in the office you can still talk to people.
[Lucy Robinson 15/11/08]

It's not altered much since I've been at Dowlow, I've only been there nine years. I like working there. It's all right. It's creating aggregates for all sorts of industries: glass, pharmaceutical, road-stone, building, all sorts. There is a sense of community working in the quarry; it's mainly local people and they don't live too far away. It's handy to home, it doesn't take me many minutes to get home and it doesn't take me many minutes to get there. It's only half a mile away.

My least favourite job is shovelling, banjo-ing. It's hard work and usually my work just consists of pressing buttons, but then, when it breaks down, you have to go banjo-ing.
[Jim Robinson 10/01/09]

I worked for a local contracting firm for seven years. It was all right. It was basically the same thing every time. Then I went working for a local firm making brake-linings. I did that for seven years.

I've been at Dowlow Quarry for thirty-one years now as an electrician. I saw an advert in the paper, applied and got the job. It was more money than what I was on where I was. It's a good bunch of blokes to work for.

My first job, in the first week up here – I started in March – I was sat in a hole by the secondary plant mending these cables in a snowstorm. And I thought, 'What the hell am I doing here?' And I'm still here thirty-one years later and I'd come from working in a factory, so it was a big shock.
[Peter Betts 10/01/09]

The biggest snow I remember was before that, in '33 when I lived up Ladmanlow. It started snowing on the Friday morning, I was working at the quarry, and it snowed all weekend till Monday. There was a snow-drift on the Leek Road, at the turn off for the Cat and Fiddle, as high as Ladmanlow Chapel. It was the end of February, but it came warm after and by the end of the week it had mostly gone. That's the worst snow I can remember.
[Percy Armitt 24/11/08]

At Tunstead my first job was what they call the picking band. We'd stand, me and another guy, either side of a conveyor belt with lime and stone going up. We picked up what they used to call 'bullheads', which was lime with bits of rock still in it. We used to pick them off and let the rest of the lime go up to the plant.
[Neil Cocker 21/01/09]

At Tunstead, on the firing floor, it was a hell of a job, that was. We used to work seven shifts, consecutive, eight-hour shifts, mornings, afternoons and nights. We worked seven shifts, then have two off, then seven shifts and have two more off. By the time you'd done three shifts, it was a month instead of three weeks. Seven shifts, that's fifty six hours, before you had any time off. Perhaps if they were short of men they'd say, 'Would you come in on your day off.' I did odd days, but I never did two. Even if you did one day that'd mean seven shifts of your own, one more is eight, one off, seven more shifts of your own, that's fifteen days out of sixteen you were working. I never had Saturday and Sunday off together, only if you were on holiday. When I came up here in '69, I retired in '72, I was here three years; people used to look at me, I was going to work Saturday afternoon and night, Sunday afternoon and night. These kilns never stopped, continuous, all week through. You got a bit extra for it, but not like they do now.
[Percy Armitt 24/11/08]

There was a camaraderie with your mates, you could go in and have a laugh, mess about in your break times, play football in your breaks, then you were back on the job. We still had a laugh whilst we were on the job, but you were there for a certain purpose.

I worked down at Tunstead for about five years and, because I lived up here, there was an opportunity opened for a job up here and I thought, 'Easier to get to work, no travelling', and I applied for the post and got it.

At Hindlow my first job was actually loading vehicles. If you like, the bottom job, then you work your way up until I'm where I am now. I've been doing my job now for just over ten years. Basically my job involves taking burnt limestone and crushing it down to any grade that you want, from talcum powder to a 100-ml lump. It's very good at Hindlow because it's a smaller workforce, you get a lot more personal contact with fitters and bosses and electricians, so it's a very close-knit community.
[Neil Cocker 21/01/09]

When I started at Dowlow in 1963 I went as a lorry driver. Then in 1972 I went partly working in the office and partly driving the minibus to bring people into the quarry. I'm not sure how long I did that for, but eventually I was made Depot Manager, probably in 1983. I was made Distribution Manager and that's the job I had until I retired.

I retired four years ago last November and I've never regretted working for the quarry at all. With hindsight it was probably the best thing I did. It's been interesting not only going from one job to another, but also promotions – I've never applied for a job.
[Gordon Riley 05/02/09]

My first job was in a laboratory. I started off as a chemist by trade. I worked in a tar-distillers near Manchester – a filthy, horrible, smelly job, but somebody had to do it. I went to work abroad for a while, I worked in the Middle East in Saudi Arabia, in the oil fields there. When I came home I just wanted the first job I could get. It happened to be a temporary job at a quarry, the one that's the RMC quarry at Dove Holes now. And from there I moved to ICI eventually.

I started off in laboratories, but when I came to ICI I took a job as an investigatory scientist. This was a job – there were a group of individuals who looked at the plant and how the plant was operating. So if we

A Getter at work on the rock face, image courtesy of Tarmac Buxton Lime & Cement

developed a new product, it was then up to the investigatory scientist to see if we could make it on the plant we'd got. If we couldn't, what plant we needed to make it.

I enjoyed the work. It's absolutely fascinating. Particularly working at one of the largest limestone quarries in Europe, really at the cutting edge of what we're doing, so that was good as well. The advert for the job didn't explain it very well and the job turned out to be far more interesting than the job I thought I was getting, and quarrying and lime production turned out to be far more complicated than I ever thought it would be.

I had to liaise with plant operators – if you're doing research on the plant you have to liaise very closely with them and get their co-operation, and it was made clear to me during the interview that might be a problem because it all depended on what personal interaction you could get with these guys. If they took a dislike to you, your job was going to be very, very difficult. I started up here at Hindlow, I was up here for nine years, and I found them to be very, very good. They were all very keen on what they were doing and also on what I was doing.

Quite a lot of the job was outside so in the depths of winter it got difficult at times, put it that way. One of the jobs that we had to do, we were doing experiments with different types of mortars and we built some test panels a metre square. They looked round for the worst area that ICI owned so that we could build these panels, and it just happened to be on the top of the tips here at Hindlow. It was the most exposed area and my job was to go up about twice a year and just see what movement there'd been in these panels. See whether the mortar had started to expand and whether the bricks were coming apart. I used to have to do that in winter, one in winter and one in summer. I can remember being up there in the depths of winter being able to do two or three readings, then having to get back into the Land Rover to thaw out, then come back and do another two or three readings and back again into the Land Rover. That sticks vividly in my memory.

The industry has changed in several ways. Safety has become much, much more stringent than it ever was. It was taken seriously when I first started in the industry. It's now taken far, far more seriously and the accident statistics show that, they show a remarkable change over the years. And I think these days we tend to get a more interested workforce, more interested in what they do. And they have more understanding of what the business does. If you go back to the '60s there tended to be an 'us and them'

mentality. The workforce were there to do a certain amount of work and the management were there to run the company. And the two were at loggerheads a fair bit of the time. Now what you tend to find is that the workforce actually understands the business, so they understand that changes are needed at times. Whereas previously, if you go back to the '60s and '70s, change was resisted because they didn't actually see how a company has to change in order to stay competitive. They've also passed quite a lot of responsibility down the chain. They've taken out a strata of management and now it's the guys on the plant that are doing a lot more responsible work now than they did. They no longer sit there at the plant and do as they're told. They are now managers in their own right.

Mechanisation has reduced the number of people working in the quarry, which has been a good thing for the company, it's been a bad thing for employment. But when you look at the sort of jobs they used to have to do, people shouldn't, in this day and age, have to do that sort of work. It was dirty, it was dangerous and it didn't do your health all that much good. And the accident statistics show that. If you look back to the 1920s, 1930s, 1940s, when they were hand-loading at the quarry face, it was killing about one person a year. Just in the ICI complex and it was very similar in the other quarries round here. You can't go on like that. And these jobs are inherently dangerous. So yes, mechanisation has speeded up what we do, it's made what we do safer and

Patent Kilns at Hindlow, 1930,
image courtesy of Tarmac Buxton Lime & Cement

made what we do cheaper. And as long as you're not throwing huge numbers of people out of work and they can't get other work, then it has to be a force for good. The environment is very important to us these days. Emissions from chimneys or incinerators, power stations, that sort of thing. There is no other technology at the moment for cleaning up these emissions other than using limestone. If we're putting effluent into rivers, generally speaking there is no other technology, other than using lime, to clean up that effluent to make it less damaging to life-forms in the river. So it is important. As I say, things may change, give it another thirty, fourty, fifty years, then maybe other technologies will be there and lime may not be used. There are things done now where lime was major, a major use, and it's hardly used at all now. Things will change as the years go on. Two hundred years' time we may not use lime or limestone at all. Who knows?

There's a photograph that shows the shaft kilns up here at Hindlow just after they were completed. The shaft kilns were built in 1929–1930. They were demolished in 1980 and replaced by modern kilns, but these were state-of-the-art technology of the time. They were built before the shaft kilns at Tunstead, so even though we now think Tunstead is at the cutting edge of what we do, back in those days Hind-low was the cutting edge because Tunstead had only just started. These kilns, they have a penthouse at the top and an enclosure about halfway up. The penthouse house at the top, they've got Buxton Lime Firm logo, the penthouse halfway down they've got ICI, and really to me that sums up the whole thing of what was happening. It was Buxton Lime Firm which had got a good solid history behind it by 1929, it had been going a long, long time, it was a major producer in the country. It's been bought by ICI, and ICI was becoming the biggest chemical company in the country and here they were, they'd just put in the most modern kilns in the country. It just shows, they're up here, at Sterndale Moor, way out of the way, but here was at the cutting edge of what was happening, certainly in the lime industry, anyway.
[Frank Emerson 10/01/09]

My hopes for the future are that nobody ever gets hurt in a quarry again and that it has a long and successful life. Not just for people working there now, but for all the local community, because it involves a lot of people, directly and indirectly. So as long as quarries stay open, local people can have a reasonable standard of living from it. As it is at the moment, a lot of places are closing all the time, especially local industry, what with Ferodo and Otters and other places. It is a very delicate time for them at the moment. So the last thing we want is for the quarry to close because it would put a lot more people out of work.
[Russell Walker 21/01/09]

TELEGRAMS:
BUXTOLIM.

TELEPHONE:
BUXTON 312.

Reply to be addressed to
The Buxton Lime Firms Company Limited
for the attention of

FROM

THE BUXTON LIME FIRMS COMPANY LIMITED,

LIME BURNERS AND QUARRY OWNERS,

ROYAL EXCHANGE,

BUXTON.

16th November, 1931.

Please note that the name of the Buxton Lime Firms Company Limited has been changed to I.C.I. (Lime) Ltd., and that the new name should now be used for all purposes.

For some time both the old and the new names will appear on the Company's notepaper and stationery as follows:-

"I.C.I. (LIME) LIMITED.
"(Formerly THE BUXTON LIME FIRMS COMPANY LIMITED.)"

but all correspondence, etc., should now be signed :-

"For I.C.I. (LIME) LIMITED "

JOHN R. MURRAY.

DELEGATE DIRECTOR.

Dowlow Quarry, Sunday 8am, 06/12/1936,
image courtesy of Lafarge Aggregates

Handloading and moving stone from the rock face, image courtesy of Tarmac Buxton Lime & Cement

Tegwyn Holman, *Loading stone at Dowlow Quarry,* 2008

Young volunteers during their research visits to Tunstead and Dowlow Quarries

Afterword

Over the course of the several months that Glassball Art Projects came to our village we learned quite a lot about the quarries that surround our houses; and the people who work there. Quarries are very important to us – not only do they provide work for the local community, but they also produce very useful materials such as lime, which can be used for numerous things. We also had the chance to look into the lives of those who work and have worked at several quarries around the area, and what they had to say was very interesting. Many of them stress just how important the quarries are and what it would be like if they didn't exist – after all, would Sterndale Moor even be here if ICI hadn't built the houses for its workers? It is unsure how long the industry will continue providing its useful service to us; sometime in the future the quarries will have to landscape their areas, and when that will be isn't easy to determine, but what is clear is that the quarries certainly have played a much-needed part in our lifestyles. The quarries that surround Sterndale Moor are a part of our community and contain the memories of those who've worked there.
[**Tegwyn Holman – young volunteer**]

We started this project not knowing a lot about our surroundings or the history of where we live. We visited three quarries, Dowlow, Hindlow and Tunstead – all on our doorstep. We learned how the quarrying industry has changed dramatically for the better and why it is so important to how we live today. The project also helped us learn about our village's heritage and we also learned many new skills along the way.
[**Lucy Robinson – young volunteer**]

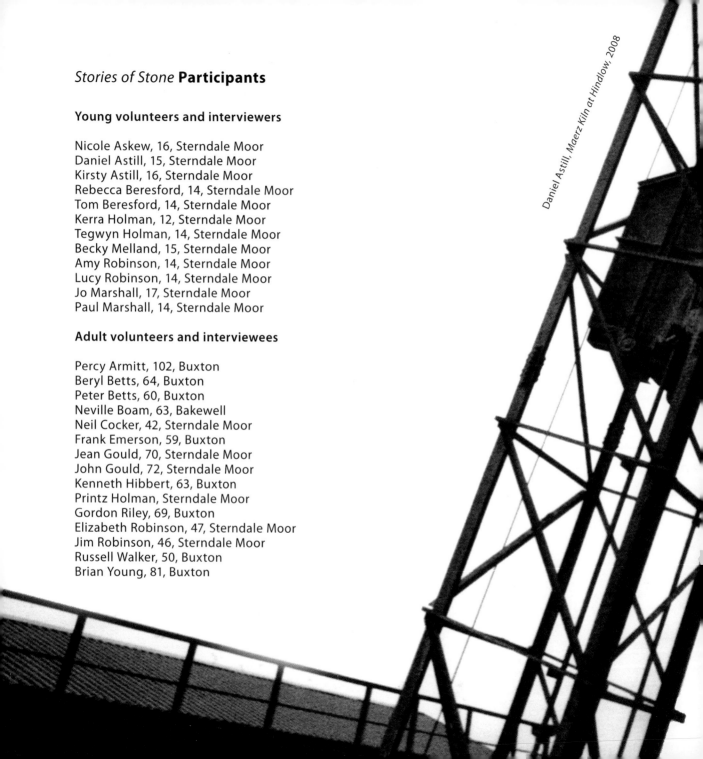

Stories of Stone **Participants**

Young volunteers and interviewers

Nicole Askew, 16, Sterndale Moor
Daniel Astill, 15, Sterndale Moor
Kirsty Astill, 16, Sterndale Moor
Rebecca Beresford, 14, Sterndale Moor
Tom Beresford, 14, Sterndale Moor
Kerra Holman, 12, Sterndale Moor
Tegwyn Holman, 14, Sterndale Moor
Becky Melland, 15, Sterndale Moor
Amy Robinson, 14, Sterndale Moor
Lucy Robinson, 14, Sterndale Moor
Jo Marshall, 17, Sterndale Moor
Paul Marshall, 14, Sterndale Moor

Adult volunteers and interviewees

Percy Armitt, 102, Buxton
Beryl Betts, 64, Buxton
Peter Betts, 60, Buxton
Neville Boam, 63, Bakewell
Neil Cocker, 42, Sterndale Moor
Frank Emerson, 59, Buxton
Jean Gould, 70, Sterndale Moor
John Gould, 72, Sterndale Moor
Kenneth Hibbert, 63, Buxton
Printz Holman, Sterndale Moor
Gordon Riley, 69, Buxton
Elizabeth Robinson, 47, Sterndale Moor
Jim Robinson, 46, Sterndale Moor
Russell Walker, 50, Buxton
Brian Young, 81, Buxton

Daniel Astill, Maerz Kiln at Hindlow, 2008